Childrens Core Collection author

STRANGE HISTORIES
THE VIKINGS

Peter Chrisp

LOOK FOR THE VIKING

Look for the carved Viking mask in boxes like this. Here you will find extra facts, stories and other interesting information about the strange world of the Vikings.

Copyright Permissions
Raintree
100 N. LaSalle St., Ste. 1200
Chicago, IL 60602

Published by Raintree, a division of Reed Elsevier, Inc.

Library of Congress Cataloging-in-Publication Data:

Chrisp, Peter.
  The Vikings / Peter Chrisp.
    v. cm. -- (Strange histories)
Includes bibliographical references and index.
Contents: Meet the Vikings -- Viking ships -- Raiding and loot -- The great army -- Viking explorers -- Trade and craft -- The Vikings at home -- Looking good -- Fun and games -- Gods and religion -- Runes and poetry -- Viking facts -- Viking words -- Viking projects.
  ISBN 0-7398-6443-2 (lib. bdg. : hardcover)
  1. Vikings--Juvenile literature. [1. Vikings.] I. Title. II. Series.
  DL65.C48 2003
  909'.0439501--dc21
                                    2002155319
Printed in Hong Kong

07 06 05 04 03
10 9 8 7 6 5 4 3 2 1

Acknowledgments
We wish to thank the following individuals and organizations for their help and assistance and for supplying material in their collections: AKG 8 top, 13 top, 16 (Jurgen Sorges), 25 top; Alamy 27 (A Woolfit); Ancient Art and Architecture Collection 5 (G Tortoli), 9 (G T Garvey), 10 (R Sheridan), 17 bottom (R Sheridan), 21 top (R Sheridan), 25 bottom (J Adlercreutz); Art Archive *back cover* (Bibliotheque des Arts Decoratifs, Paris/Dagli Orti), 1 (Bibliotheque des Arts Decoratifs, Paris/Dagli Orti), 3 (Historiska Museet, Oslo/Dagli Orti), 6 (Bibliotheque des Arts Decoratifs, Paris/Dagli Orti), 7 top (Historiska Museet, Oslo/Dagli Orti); Canadian Tourist Commission 12; Corbis 17 top (Wolfgang Kaehler); C M Dixon 7 bottom, 8 bottom, 18 bottom, 19 bottom, 20, 21 bottom, 22 top, 23; Hunterian Museum, University of Glasgow 19 top left and top right; MPM Images 28 (Daniel Rogers); Topham Picturepoint 2 (Ted Spiegel), 11 bottom (Ted Spiegel), 15 bottom, 22 bottom (Ted Spiegel), 29 (Ted Spiegel); Werner Forman Archive *front cover* (Viking Ship Museum, Bygdoy), 4 (Viking Ship Museum, Bygdoy), 11 top (British Museum, London), 13 bottom, 18 top (Statens Historiska Museum, Stockholm), 26; York Archaeological Trust 15 top. Artwork by Michael Posen.

◄ *Vikings raided British and Irish monasteries in search of treasures, like this bronze- and silver-plated casket.*

CONTENTS

▶ *This richly decorated gold and bronze weather vane was fixed to the prow (front) or mast of a Viking warship.*

MEET THE VIKINGS

This is a book about men and women with strange names, such as Thorstein Cod-Biter, Ulf the Unwashed, Einar Belly-Shaker, and Aud the Deep-Minded.

These were the real names of people from Norway, Denmark, and Sweden, who lived over a thousand years ago. Today, we call the people of these northern lands "Vikings," a word that probably once meant "raider." Many people still think of Vikings as simply fierce raiders, but there was much more to them than that. They were also farmers, explorers, traders, and skilled artisans.

The age of the Vikings lasted from about 780 to 1100 C.E. In these years Vikings left their homelands and set off on great journeys in all directions.

▲ *The red shading on this map shows the lands the Vikings came from.*

▶ *This fierce-looking Viking was carved on the wooden post of a cart found in a grave in Norway.*

4

The Norwegians sailed west across the Atlantic Ocean to explore and find new lands in which to settle. Danes and Norwegians crossed the North Sea to raid and invade the rich lands of Great Britain, Ireland, France, and Germany. Meanwhile, Swedish Vikings made trading journeys east and south along the rivers of Russia.

▼ *In their homelands, such as Norway, the Vikings usually lived close to water, along **fjords,** or near deep inlets leading to the sea.*

ODD NAMES

Vikings did not write books, so much of what we know about them comes from accounts written by their enemies, the people whose lands they raided. Yet they did remember their past through poems and stories. In the 13th and 14th centuries, these were finally written down in books called **Sagas.** It is from the Sagas that we know that the Vikings liked giving each other strange nicknames. These were often jokes. For example, a big, strong, powerful man called Thorbjorn was called Thorbjorn the Feeble.

VIKING SHIPS

One of the strangest Viking customs was to bury their dead inside ships and boats. Nobody knows why they did this.

Perhaps they thought of death as the start of a journey to another world. A Viking would think it quite natural to make such a journey by ship. Whatever the reason, because of this custom we can still see Viking ships today.

THE GOKSTAD SHIP

The Gokstad ship was built of overlapping oak planks and was 76 feet (23.3 meters) long. It was known to carry a crew of at least 64 men, because this was the number of shields found on board. A replica of the ship, built in 1893, sailed from Norway to Canada in 28 days.

▼ *A fleet of dragon-headed Viking longships races across the sea.*

The best-preserved Viking ship burial was found in 1881 at Gokstad in Norway. The Gokstad ship was a *langskip*, or **longship,** a narrow, slim warship built for speed. It was strong enough to cross stormy seas but light enough to travel up shallow rivers or to be dragged up onto a beach. With ships like this, Vikings could go almost anywhere.

Vikings loved their ships and gave them names, such as "long serpent" or "sea snake." The *prows* (fronts) were decorated with the carved heads of snakes, dragons, or other fierce animals. To a Viking warrior, sailing into battle might have felt like riding on the back of a fierce dragon.

Although the Gokstad ship looks plain today, it may once have been brightly colored. There is evidence for this on the wall hanging called the **Bayeux Tapestry,** which shows longships painted in colored stripes with patterned sails.

▶ *Rich and powerful Vikings decorated the prows and masts of their ships with beautiful metal weather vanes that shone in the sun.*

▼ *This snarling animal head was found in a Viking ship burial in Norway.*

RAIDING AND LOOT

At the beginning of the Viking age, there were many **monasteries** around the coasts of Britain and Ireland. These were places where Christian holy men, called monks, spent their days worshiping God.

The monks built monasteries near the ocean, often on little islands, because they felt safe there. They never expected to be attacked by strange men in **longships.**

The first and most shocking raid on a monastery took place in the year 793. The monastery of Lindisfarne, one of the holiest places in Britain, was attacked. Some of the monks were killed, while others were taken away to be slaves.

▲ *Vikings prized their swords and gave them names like "Leg-biter" and "Skull-crusher."*

◀ *This carving from Lindisfarne is thought to show Viking raiders, armed with swords and battle-axes.*

WHAT DID THEY DO WITH THE LOOT?

Viking warriors looked up to people who were generous and would only follow leaders who regularly gave away their wealth. Such chieftains and kings were called "ring-givers." This meant that, to win power and keep his men's loyalty, a Viking leader needed a constant supply of wealth. This was a good reason to keep raiding Britain and Ireland.

▼ *In response to Viking attacks, Irish monks began to build tall towers so that they could look out for the raiders and take shelter.*

From a Viking point of view, Lindisfarne was a perfect place to attack. It was right next to the ocean and the monks who lived there were holy men who did not have weapons or know how to fight back. They also had many treasures, such as gilded Bibles and jeweled **shrines.**

Raids did not always go according to plan. A year after Lindisfarne was attacked, a fleet of Viking longships raided the nearby monastery at Jarrow. Before they could sail home, their fleet was hit by a violent storm. Some of the longships sank and many men drowned. The survivors who swam ashore were killed by the angry English.

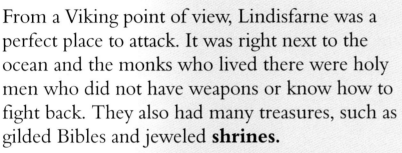
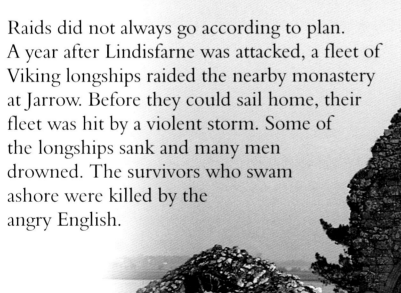

THE GREAT ARMY

According to the **Sagas,** a Viking raider called Ragnar Hairy-Breeches was captured by the English king, Aella of York. Aella had Ragnar thrown to his death in a pit filled with poisonous snakes.

Back in Denmark Ragnar had a son, Ivar the Boneless. Ivar decided to avenge his father's death. He raised a great army and invaded England. Ivar captured and killed Aella.

The story of Ivar was written long after the events it describes took place and most of it was probably made up for entertainment. Yet there was a Viking called Ivar. He was one of the leaders of the Great Army of Danes, which invaded England in the year 865. Aella of York was killed by these Vikings.

▲ *This Swedish silver pendant, showing the face of a warrior or a god, might have been made from silver taken from England.*

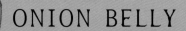 ONION BELLY

When a Viking was wounded in the stomach, he was given a meal of oatmeal porridge flavored with onions. If his wound smelled like onions, it meant that his guts had been pierced and he would probably die. If there was no smell, it meant that he might recover, so his wounds would be bandaged.

The arrival of the Great Army showed that the Vikings were getting more organized. For years wealth from raiding trips had been pouring into the Viking homelands, and more and more men wanted to take part in the raids. By the 850s Viking fleets of hundreds of ships were setting off across the North Sea. They sailed up rivers, such as the Rhine in Germany and the Seine in France, to attack big towns.

◀ *A Viking coin. The Vikings knew that England was a land of great wealth. Unlike early Viking rulers, English kings minted their own silver coins.*

The Vikings in the Great Army were not raiders. They had come to conquer the land of England and to stay there. They spent the next fourteeen years moving around the country, fighting and beating one English king after another. Eventually, in 878, they made peace with the English king, Alfred the Great. The English and the Vikings shared the land between them.

▼ *This carving shows a great Viking war fleet, like the one that landed in England in 865. The ships' prows are decorated with dragon heads and weather vanes.*

VIKING EXPLORERS

Perhaps the bravest Vikings were the explorers who sailed west into the North Atlantic Ocean, looking for new lands. They reached, and named, the Faeroe Islands, Iceland, and Greenland. From Greenland they sailed on to North America, which they called Vinland (Wine Land).

The stories of Viking voyages of exploration were remembered in Iceland and written down in the **Sagas.** According to the Sagas, Iceland, Greenland, and North America were all found by accident by Vikings blown off course on voyages to other places. When they returned home and described their discoveries, they gave others the idea to find and settle in the new lands.

CRYSTAL GAZING

Vikings found their way at sea by the height of the sun, which told them how far to the north or south they were. On cloudy days when the sun was hidden, they may have used a crystal called a "sun stone," which is mentioned in the Sagas. They held this crystal up, moving it until the light seen through it changed color. This showed where the sun was.

◀ *Today in Newfoundland, people reenact the way of life of the first Vikings who settled there.*

In the 860s a man called Floki Raven set out to find Iceland. Floki earned his nickname because he took ravens with him on his voyage. Since birds in the air can see farther than men on a ship, Floki knew that they would spot land before he did. So he released the birds and when they could not see land, they flew back to his ship. When they did see land they flew off, with Floki sailing after them.

Until recently the only evidence that Vikings reached North America was in the Sagas. However, in the 1960s **archaeologists** discovered a group of Viking turf houses in Newfoundland, just off the coast of North America. This discovery proved that the Sagas were telling the truth.

▲ The explorer Leif Eriksson was the first European to land in North America. Here he is shown sighting the new land.

▼ When they reached a new coast, Viking explorers would drop a simple wooden anchor weighted with a rock.

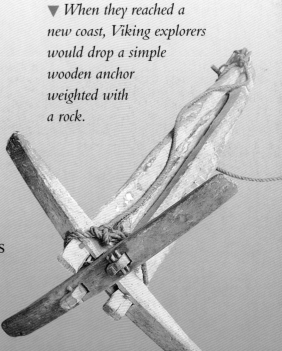

TRADE AND CRAFT

T he Vikings were the most successful traders of their time. They had the best ships and were willing to travel great distances if there was a chance to gain wealth. Viking traders carried goods far and wide, from Lapland in the icy north to Greece and the hot lands of the Arabs in the south.

Trade flourished because Vikings settled in many different places yet kept in touch with their homelands. Merchant ships from Norway made regular journeys across the sea to Iceland and Greenland, carrying timber to sell. They exchanged this for wool, furs, and wild **falcons.** Viking trade led to the growth of towns, such as Dublin and Limerick in Ireland, York in England, and Hedeby in Denmark.

▼ *This map shows the trade routes used by the Vikings.*

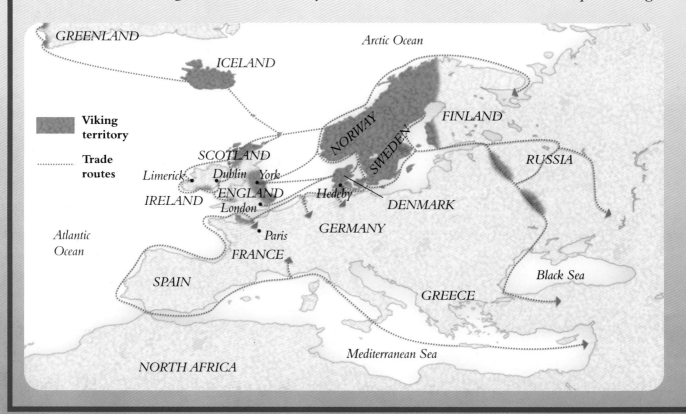

GREENLAND

ICELAND

Arctic Ocean

Viking territory

.... **Trade routes**

FINLAND

NORWAY

SWEDEN

RUSSIA

SCOTLAND

Limerick   Dublin   York

ENGLAND   Hedeby

IRELAND   London   DENMARK

Atlantic Ocean

GERMANY

Paris

FRANCE

Black Sea

SPAIN

GREECE

Mediterranean Sea

NORTH AFRICA

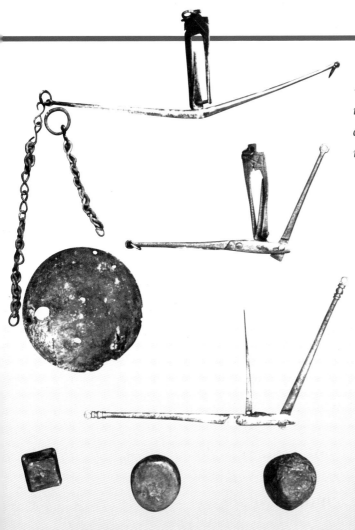

◄ *Viking merchants traded using silver, valued by weight rather than by different types of coin. The silver was weighed with folding scales like these.*

▼ *Viking craftspeople loved to carve strange animals out of wood, to decorate items of furniture and tools.*

Viking traders would buy and sell anything, even people. Ireland was a big source of **thralls,** or slaves. These were Irish people captured by Vikings in raids. Many Irish men and women ended up as thralls, doing the hard work on farms in places like Iceland. In Iceland a big, strong male thrall was said to cost 24 cows. A woman, who was not as strong, cost just eight cows.

THE VIKINGS AT HOME

Think of having to live in a house with several other people, all sharing one big room. Houses like this were common in Viking times. The big room had benches around the walls and a central fireplace for warmth, cooking, and light.

Viking families sat around the fire in the evenings and slept on the benches at night, wrapped up in furs and blankets. In the cold northern lands, it was more important to keep warm than to have your own private bedroom.

In Sweden, Denmark, England, and Ireland, people lived in villages and towns. In Norway, the Scottish Isles, Iceland, and Greenland, they lived in single farmhouses, often miles from their nearest neighbor. The only time they might meet their neighbors was at a big open-air meeting called a **Thing.** The Thing, which was held regularly, was a place to do business, arrange marriages, sort out quarrels, and try legal cases.

▼ *This modern reconstruction of a farm in Iceland shows the typical long and narrow shape of a Viking home.*

▲ *We know the shape of Viking houses thanks to archaeological remains. This long house was found at Jarshof in England.*

▲ *This reconstruction at Jorvik (York, England) shows how cluttered a Viking home must have been.*

GULL LIGHTING

Seabirds, such as gulls, have a lot of oil in their bodies. Vikings caught gulls and boiled them in a pot, collecting the oil that floated on top of the water. They used this oil to light their homes, burning it in lamps carved from soft **soapstone.**

LOOKING GOOD

Perhaps we think of Vikings as shaggy-haired and filthy. In fact, Viking men and women spent a lot of time on their appearance.

An English writer complained that Viking men were popular with English women because, unlike English men, they regularly changed their clothes, combed their hair, and took a bath on Saturdays. Swedish Vikings even called Saturday "bath day."

We do know that Vikings combed their hair regularly because combs, made from animal bone, are common finds at Viking sites. One good reason for combing the hair was to get rid of fleas and head lice, which must have been common in Viking houses.

▲*Viking men and women wore jewelry, such as this dragon-headed arm ring.*

GRAVE CLUES

Most of what we know about Viking clothes comes from items found in graves. Since cloth hardly ever survives, **archaeologists** have to figure out how people dressed from other clues, such as the position on a skeleton of metal brooches or buckles. Two large oval brooches are usually found by the shoulders of female skeletons, showing us where these were worn.

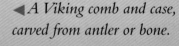

◀*A Viking comb and case, carved from antler or bone.*

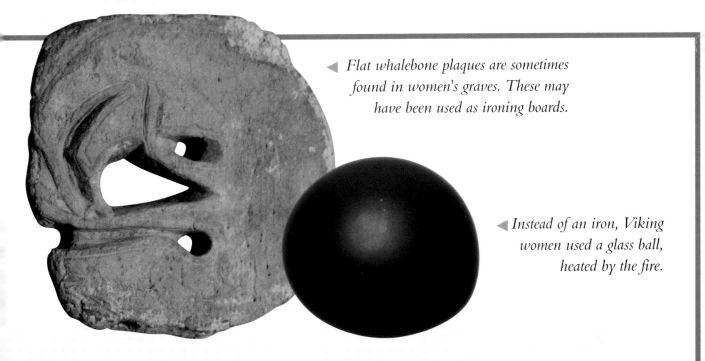

Flat whalebone plaques are sometimes found in women's graves. These may have been used as ironing boards.

Instead of an iron, Viking women used a glass ball, heated by the fire.

The strangest clue about how Vikings looked comes from an Arab merchant called Al-Tartushi. He visited Hedeby in Denmark in about 950 and wrote that the men and women there wore eye makeup. "When they use it," he wrote, "the beauty of both men and women increases."

Women wore a long-sleeved linen or woolen tunic that reached their ankles. On top they had a woolen apron-dress held in place by a pair of big oval brooches. There was often a chain or string of beads between the brooches. Without handbags or pockets, this chain was a useful place to hang small items such as keys, combs, or scissors.

Wet soil sometimes preserves leather clothing, such as this Viking shoe.

Men wore pants, a short tunic, and a cloak fastened at one shoulder with a brooch. Swords, knives, and other belongings dangled from their leather belts. From carvings, we know that Viking men grew beards and moustaches, but often kept their hair short at the back and sides.

Fun and Games

In the northern lands where the Vikings lived, the days are short in winter. People spent the long, dark nights indoors, sitting around the fire.

They made their own entertainment, playing board games, telling stories, inventing poems and riddles, and singing songs. Viking songs were not to everyone's taste. Al-Tartushi, an Arab merchant who visited Denmark, wrote: "Nothing can compare with the horrible singing of these people. It's even worse than the barking of dogs!"

There were many different board games. The best known was called **Hnefatafl,** or king's table. It was like a battle in which a king and his warriors were surrounded by a larger enemy army. The king, who began at the center, had to find a way through the enemy pieces and escape to the side of the board. You can find out how to play *hnefatafl* on page 30.

▼ *Chess became more popular at the end of the Viking age. These beautiful chessmen, carved from Norwegian walrus ivory, were found on the Scottish Isle of Lewis.*

This wooden gaming board, found in Ireland, could have been used for hnefatafl. *The pieces would be pegs placed in the holes.*

When it was sunny, people played outdoor games such as soccer with an inflated pig's bladder. Men and boys enjoyed trials of strength and skill, including swimming, wrestling, or simply throwing large boulders around. One game was like "monkey in the middle." Four people stood in a square, throwing a rolled-up bearskin to each other, while a fifth person tried to catch it.

In Iceland and Norway, the most popular Viking sport was horse fighting. Two stallions (male horses) were made to fight each other while a crowd of onlookers gambled money on which horse would win. A good fighting horse was very valuable.

▼ *Horse fighting is shown on this carved stone. The owners drive their horses forward with sticks.*

GODS AND RELIGION

The Vikings worshiped many gods who had all sorts of strange powers. The most important were Odin, god of war and magic; Frey, god of the sun and crops; and Thor, god of thunder, storms, and lightning.

Like modern superheroes, each Viking god had his own special abilities and magic equipment. Frey, for example, owned a magic ship called *Skidbladnir*. This was big enough to hold all the other gods, yet could be folded up and carried in a little bag.

▲ *A bronze statuette of Thor, god of thunder, whose magical hammer is growing out of his beard!*

◀ *A Viking burial ground in Denmark, with the stone outlines of ships over each grave. Like the buried ships, these graves suggest that Vikings saw death as the start of a voyage to the next world.*

Thor was a red-bearded god who rode across the sky in a chariot pulled by two goats. He was armed with a mighty hammer called *Mjollnir* ("crusher"). Thor was a friendly god, believed to bring good luck. On sea journeys people asked Thor for good weather, and many Vikings named their children after him, with names such as Thorvald, Thorbjorn, and Thora. Nobody was ever named after Odin, who was a much more frightening god.

Vikings won their gods' help by making sacrifices, or offerings, to them. Horses, dogs, goats, and sometimes even people were killed as sacrifices. Their blood was offered to the gods, and their bodies were hung from trees or poles. Before a battle, Vikings sometimes promised the whole enemy army as a sacrifice to Odin. By doing this, they hoped that he would help them kill as many enemies as possible.

The Vikings soon discovered that most other Europeans were Christians. Many Vikings began to worship Christ, too, at first as just another useful god. Over time, the worship of the old gods died out. Yet people still enjoyed telling stories of the adventures of Thor and the other gods.

WHAT'S IN A NAME?

Four days of the week are named after Viking gods: Tuesday (Ty's day), Wednesday (Odin's day), Thursday (Thor's day) and Friday (Frey's day). These were not named by Vikings but by the **Anglo-Saxons,** or English. Before they became Christians, the Anglo-Saxons worshiped the same gods as the Vikings.

▼ *This carving shows Odin's eight-legged horse, Sleipnir. It carried Vikings killed in battle to Odin's hall, Valhalla.*

Runes and Poetry

Although they did not write books, Vikings had a simple writing system that used letters called **runes.** These were believed to have been discovered by Odin and were also thought to have magical powers.

Vikings sometimes used runes in spells to try to make enemies fall ill or to help sick people get better. To heal a wound, a spell might be scratched on a piece of bone and wrapped in a bandage around the injury.

People also used runes for everyday purposes, such as writing their names on a brooch or a sword. Sometimes people simply wrote their names on walls. Viking names have been found scratched on statues and churches in Greece and inside ancient stone tombs in the **Orkneys.** Like graffiti artists of today, Vikings liked leaving their names behind wherever they went.

WAVE HORSES AND SEA DEER

In their poetry Vikings liked to come up with unusual ways of describing everyday things. A ship could be called a "sea deer," a "wave horse" or a "sea bench." The sky might be "bird world," while the sea could be "whale home." Can you think of any other names for the sky and the sea?

▼ *There were sixteen runes, all made of straight lines, which made them easy to carve or scratch on bone, stone, or wood. (The letters in our alphabet that sound most like the runes are shown below.)*

F U TH A R K H N I A S T B M L R

In the Viking homelands, there are over 3,000 standing stones carved with runes praising dead men and women, set up by their friends and relatives. Those for men say things like, "He was the terror of men, and met his death in the East." Women were celebrated for their skills running the house and farm. A typical stone says, "She was the most skillful girl in Hadeland." Every Viking man or woman hoped to be remembered well after death.

▲ *Viking rune stones often include pictures as well as writing. Here you can see a warrior thrusting his sword through the line of runes.*

Another way of being remembered was in a poem. Viking rulers had their own skalds, or poets, whose job was to invent poems praising their lord's generosity and bravery. Ordinary people also thought up poems to entertain their family and friends.

▼ *This is one of a group of fifteen standing stones at Anundshog in Sweden. The runes say, "Folkvid raised all these stones in memory of his son, Anund's brother."*

Viking Facts

Here is a selection of interesting facts about the strange world of the Vikings.

VIKINGS TODAY

Although the Viking age ended almost a thousand years ago, in some ways the Vikings are still with us today. Scientific tests have shown that many people living in the British Isles are descended from Viking settlers. In the **Orkneys,** for example, more than three-quarters of the population is of Norwegian descent.

VIKING WORDS

In England Viking settlers and English people lived side by side, and English speakers eventually picked up Scandinavian words. Hundreds of the everyday English words are really Viking words. These include "happy," "law," "call," "take," "knife," "ugly," "fellow," "sky," "skin," "husband," "they," "window," and "anger."

▼ *Icelanders claim to have the world's oldest Congress. Their Viking* Althing *(assembly) first met on this plain in the year 930. Iceland's* Althing *now meets in the capital, Reykjavik.*

*Every January Shetlanders celebrate a fire festival, "Up-Helly-Aa," and burn a **longship** to remind them of their Viking past.*

YORKSHIRE SAYINGS

In places densely settled by Scandinavians, such as Yorkshire in Britain, there are even more Viking words. These include the Yorkshire greeting or warning "hey up!" and words such as "gawp" (to stare at) and "dollop" (soft lump).

SCANDINAVIAN PLACES

If you look at a map of Britain, you will find hundreds of Scandinavian place names telling us where Vikings once lived. The most common end in "by," meaning homestead or village. Look also for "thorpe" (new village), "holm" (island), "thwaite" (clearing), "wick" (harbor), "dale" (valley), and "ness" (headland). Such place names often include the name of a Viking settler. Grimsby, for example, was a place where a Viking called Grim once had his homestead. Scunthorpe was the village of a Viking called Skuma.

FATHER'S NAME

In Iceland people are even closer to their Viking past. Their language is much like that of the first Viking settlers, and they still use their father's first name as a surname, just as the Vikings did. For example, Gudrun the daughter of Erik would be called Gudrun Eriksdottir. Her brother Olaf would be called Olaf Erikson.

VIKING WORDS

This glossary explains some of the words used in this book that you might not have seen before.

Anglo-Saxons the name of the Germanic people who invaded England in the 5th and 6th centuries and were living there at the time of the Norman Conquest

archaeologist someone who digs up remains from earlier times to find out what life was like in the past

Bayeux Tapestry a 230-foot (70-meter) long wall hanging, made to celebrate the Norman Conquest of England in 1066

falcon bird used in hunting

fjord deep inlet leading to the sea

Hnefatafl "King's table," a Viking board game

▼ *A scene from the Bayeux Tapestry showing the Norman invaders defeating the Anglo-Saxon army in 1066.*

This casket shrine once held bones of Saint Columba, an Irish monk who preached Christianity in Scotland. Many shrines like this were stolen by Vikings, who threw the bones away as "worthless [garbage]."

longship a Viking warship, so-called because it was long and slim. It was built for speed.

monastery place where holy men, called monks, lived and spent their time worshiping God

Normans Vikings who had settled in France

Orkneys islands off the northeast tip of Scotland

rune Viking letter, designed for carving. Runes were used on things like gravestones, swords, and jewelry. They were believed to have magical powers.

Saga a long story, recording events in Viking history. Most Sagas were written in Iceland between the 13th and 14th centuries.

Scandinavia a name for the Viking homelands of Norway, Sweden, and Denmark. People from these lands are also called Scandinavians.

shrine box holding the bones of saints

soapstone soft rock

Thing a big open-air meeting, where Vikings discussed important business and made decisions, such as in law cases

thrall a slave—someone owned by someone else and bought or sold as property

VIKING PROJECTS

Now that you've read about the strange world of the Vikings, why not begin your own project? There are many different things you can make, do, and find out. You could learn the **runic** alphabet (see page 24) and write your own name using the characters. You might use cardboard to make a **longship,** a helmet, or a Viking house. See if you can learn more about Viking explorers and heroes at your local library or on the Internet.

PLAY HNEFATAFL

Why not make your own board and pieces for **Hnefatafl,** the Viking board game? Use a piece of square cardboard for the board. Draw straight lines across it to divide it into seven rows of seven squares. Make the game pieces from modeling clay. There should be nine white pieces, including the king, which should be larger, and sixteen black pieces. Set up the board like the picture at the top of this page.

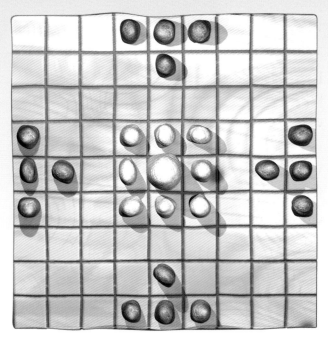

▲ *This picture shows how the board is set up at the start of a game.*

▼ *The white king is the largest piece.*

King

How to play

The players take turns, moving one piece at a time. White moves first. A piece moves any number of squares in a straight line, up, down, or from side to side, like a rook in chess. A player captures an enemy piece by getting two pieces into squares on either side of it. The captured piece is removed from the board. Black wins by surrounding the king on four sides. White wins if the king can reach one of the sides of the board.

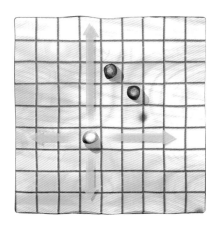

◀ *Pieces move in straight lines.*

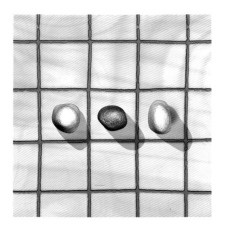

◀ *The black piece has been captured by the two white pieces.*

▶ *The white king has been surrounded by four black pieces. Black has won the game.*

INDEX